THE HUMAN MACHINE

THE
POWER PACK

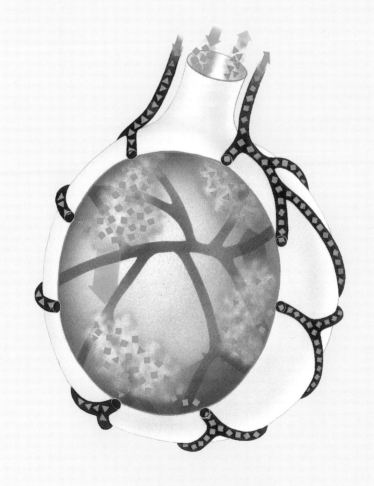

Sarah Angliss

Illustrations by Graham Rosewarne

Thameside Press

Distributed in the United States by
Smart Apple Media
123 South Broad Street
Mankato, Minnesota 56001

Text copyright © Sarah Angliss 1999

Editor: Susie Brooks
Designer: Helen James
Educational consultant: Carol Ballard

Printed in Singapore

ISBN 1-929298-19-6
Library of Congress Catalog Card Number 99-73410

10 9 8 7 6 5 4 3 2 1

Words in **bold** are explained in the glossary on pages 30 and 31.

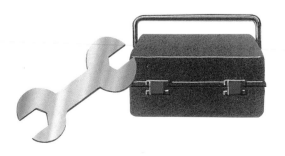

CONTENTS

THE POWER PACK

Think of your body as an amazing machine— a human machine. Every machine needs a power pack to keep it running. Yours is made up of your lungs, airways, heart, and blood. These parts work together to deliver life-giving supplies all around your body and remove unwanted waste from every cell.

Look out for diagrams like this throughout the book. They show where each part of your power pack is found in your body.

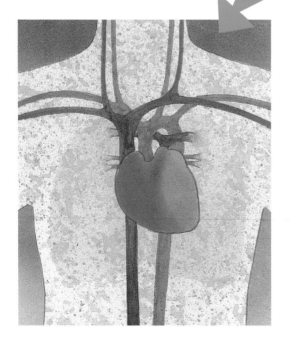

Power play?

Your **heart**, **lungs**, and **blood vessels** don't really look like this! The main pictures in this book are drawn with a bit of imagination. But look at them carefully —they show how each part of your power pack works.

Breath of life

The moment you were born, you took in a huge gulp of air to fill your lungs. You'll continue breathing until the time you die. Your breathing system is part of your body's power pack. It supplies you with **oxygen**—a gas from the air that you can't live without.

Circuit supplies

Your heart is pumping blood around your body all the time. This enables your blood to deliver oxygen to all your body's **cells**. Your blood also supplies your body with the **nutrients** it needs to fuel and defend itself—and to patch itself up. The way blood moves around your body is called your **circulation**.

Gas works

Your cells need oxygen to break down the nutrients in your blood, releasing energy and the chemicals they need to work, repair themselves, and grow. As your cells work, they produce a lot of waste—mainly water and a gas called **carbon dioxide**. These are cleared away from your lungs and removed from your body when you breathe out.

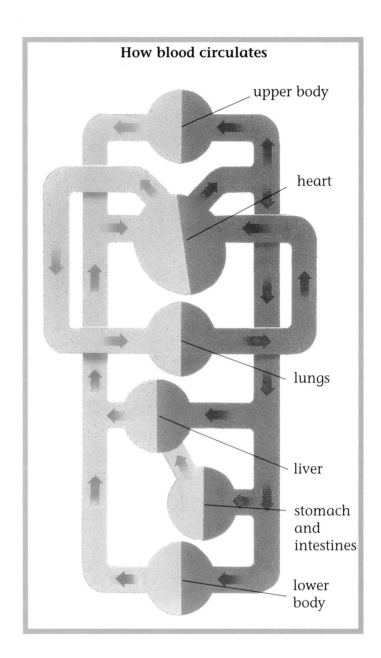

How blood circulates

upper body

heart

lungs

liver

stomach and intestines

lower body

Breakdown!

Just like the engine of any machine, the human power pack can break down. Often these parts can mend themselves, but sometimes they need a helping hand. Tool boxes like this one tell you what happens when part of your power pack needs repair.

5

AIR PREPARERS

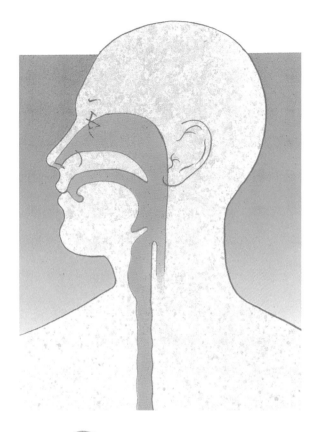

The human machine has its own air conditioning system. This makes the air you breathe in ready for your power pack to use.

The air around you can be dusty, dry, and cold. If it reached your **lungs** in this state, they might not work very well. That's why you need a nose and **nasal cavity**. These special parts filter, warm, and dampen the air as you breathe it in.

Furry filters

You usually breathe in air through your nostrils. Just inside these two openings are lots of little hairs. As air is sucked in, unwanted bits and pieces catch on these hairs, like leaves in a drain.

Hairy hollow

Your nasal cavity is a warm hollow, hidden behind your nose. It heats the air up to the right temperature for your body.

Millions of tiny hairs, called **cilia**, line the nasal cavity walls. Cilia waft backwards when you breathe in, sweeping up germs and fine pieces of dust that escaped the longer hairs inside your nose.

dirt catches in nose hairs

What a blast!

A sneeze is a quick way to clean out your body's air conditioning system. You feel the urge to sneeze if dust or mucus irritates the lining of your nasal cavity. When you sneeze, you force a huge blast of air out of your nose. This usually shoots out the cause of the tickle—ideally into a handkerchief or tissue!

Emergency entrance

You probably breathe through your nose most of the time—but if it gets blocked you can breathe through your mouth instead. Unfortunately though, your mouth isn't hairy like your nose, so it can't give incoming air the same clean sweep.

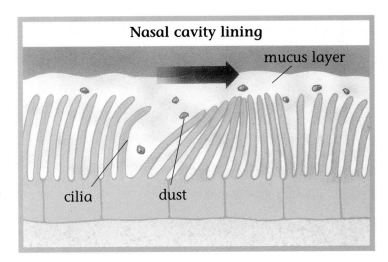

Nasal cavity lining

mucus layer

cilia   dust

Slimy sweep

The lining of your nasal cavity makes a slime, called **mucus**, that covers the cilia. It also makes mucus for your nose. Dust and germs trapped by the hairs get caught up in this mucus.

When your nose runs, some mucus comes out through your nostrils, taking dirt away with it. Your cilia brush back more dusty mucus towards a chute, called your throat, or **pharynx**. From there it slips down your food pipe, into your stomach, when you swallow.

Fleshy flap

As you swallow, a fleshy trap door, called your **epiglottis**, closes over the entrance to your airway, or **trachea**, to stop the mucus heading for your lungs. When you're not swallowing, the door stays open to let any cleaned, warmed, and filtered air through.

cilia sweep up fine dust and germs

dusty mucus moves back towards throat

epiglottis lets prepared air through to trachea

mucus slips down food pipe

BULGING BUZZER

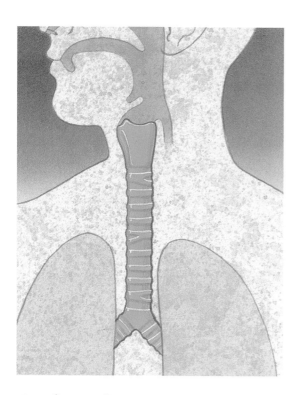

Newly cleaned and warmed air moves down a stiff branching tube called your trachea. At the top of this tube is a bulging, buzzing box called your larynx. This is where the sound of your voice comes from.

Active airway

Your **trachea** takes air from your **pharynx** toward your **lungs**, where the **oxygen** is then passed into your blood. But you need air for more than oxygen —you also need it to speak. You make sounds when air passes through your **larynx**. This tough box at the top of your trachea houses your buzzing **vocal cords**.

Your vocal cords are two strong sheets of skin that stretch across your larynx like a pair of drumskins. When you're not speaking, they stay slightly apart and remain still so that air can pass silently through your trachea, to and from your lungs. But when you talk, they spring into action.

air brushes against vocal cords as you breathe out

larynx houses vocal cords

air passes through trachea

Shaking sounds

When you want to make a speaking sound, your vocal cords draw together, cutting into the air that's passing between them. The moving air makes them wobble to and fro hundreds of times every second, like two drumskins that have been hit. This shaking action makes a sound. You can make the sound into words by moving your tongue and lips in different ways.

If your vocal cords tighten, they wobble faster so you make a higher sound. If air passes between them more quickly, they wobble more so you make a sound that's louder.

Strange silence

*Have you ever lost your voice? If your larynx becomes infected —by a bad cold, for instance— it can swell or clog with **mucus**. This stops your vocal cords from vibrating so freely. They might be able to wobble just enough to give you a croaky voice, but if they seize up altogether, you can't make any sound at all.*

vocal cords wobble to and fro to make a sound

Tough tube

A ring of **cartilage** around your larynx protects it. The bulge it sometimes makes in your neck is called your Adam's apple. Your trachea is stiffened with ridges of cartilage all the way down its front and sides. This stops it from collapsing, making a clear passageway for the air you breathe in and out. At the bottom, your trachea branches into two **bronchi**—the airways that lead to your lungs.

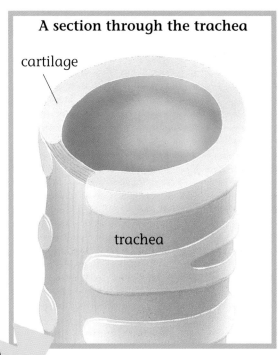

A section through the trachea

cartilage

trachea

A quiet word

Your vocal cords don't need to wobble to make every sound that you speak. When you whisper, for instance, the quiet hissing sounds you make come from air puffing through your mouth. Sounds like "t" and "sh" are also produced by your mouth in this way.

AIR SPONGES

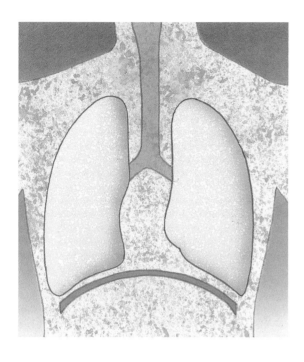

*T*wo spongy bags—your lungs—take in and puff out the air you breathe. A sheet of muscle called your diaphragm plunges up and down below your lungs, forcing the air in and out.

If you breathe in and out while you look in the mirror, you'll see your chest grow and shrink in size. That's because your **lungs** are filling up with air, then emptying again.

Pumping force

Air wouldn't move in and out of your lungs unless it was forced to. That's why you need a **diaphragm**. This domed sheet of muscle works a bit like a plunger. It moves up and down below your lungs, making you breathe in and out by forcing the spongy bags to change in size.

Making space

Your diaphragm stretches right across the base of your rib cage. When you **inhale**, it tightens and pulls downwards. At the same time, muscles between your ribs pull your rib cage outwards. This makes extra space inside your chest. Your lungs expand to fill the space, drawing air into them as they grow.

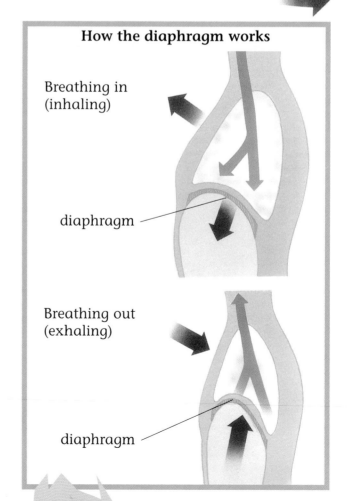

How the diaphragm works

Breathing in (inhaling)

diaphragm

Breathing out (exhaling)

diaphragm

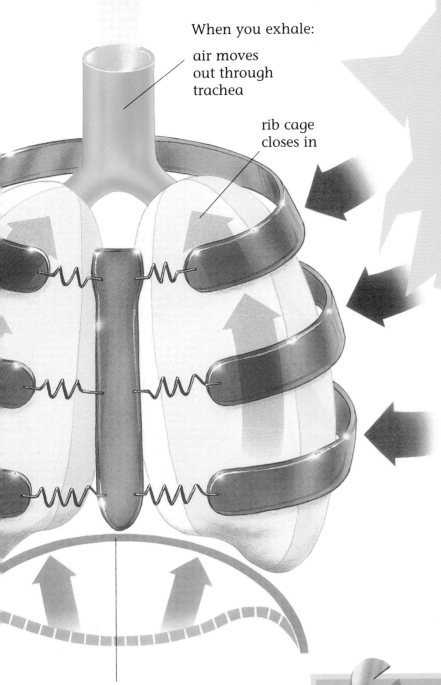

When you exhale:

air moves
out through
trachea

rib cage
closes in

diaphragm springs
upwards to force
air out of lungs

In control

Most of the time, you breathe
in and out without noticing—
breathing is an automatic action,
controlled by your brain. But you
can switch off automatic if you
need to breathe in a special way.
For instance, you can hold your
breath for a few seconds if you
swim underwater—or if you
want to avoid a nasty smell.

Closing in

When you need to breathe out,
or **exhale**, muscles in your chest
relax. Your diaphragm springs back
upwards and your rib cage closes
in. This makes your chest space
smaller, squashing your lungs.

Air is pushed out of your lungs as
they shrink, just like toothpaste is
squeezed out of a tube. It is forced
back up through your **bronchi** and
trachea, then breathed out of your
nose or mouth.

Smooth surface

A slippery skin on the outside
of your lungs keeps them well
oiled. This makes sure they
can grow and shrink easily
with every breath.

Medical mystery

*Hiccups sound really silly—and they seem
to be pretty pointless too. You hiccup when
your diaphragm gets the jitters, tightening
suddenly so it forces a burst of air through
your **vocal cords**. Anything from hunger
to fear can trigger an attack
of hiccups. No one has any
idea what hiccups are for.*

11

CENTRAL EXCHANGE

Find out more about capillaries on pages 20-21.

carbon dioxide from blood in capillaries moves into air in alveoli

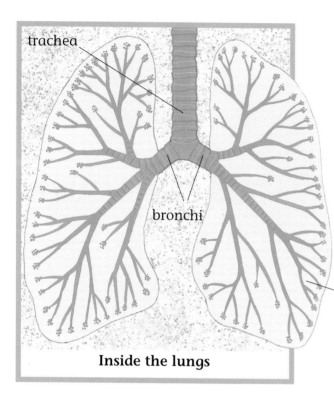

trachea

bronchi

Inside the lungs

Inside your air sponges, the gases you breathe are sorted out by tiny filtering sacks. These are called your alveoli.

Once air reaches your **lungs**, the **oxygen** in it needs to enter your blood so it can be delivered to every living **cell** in your body.

bronchioles

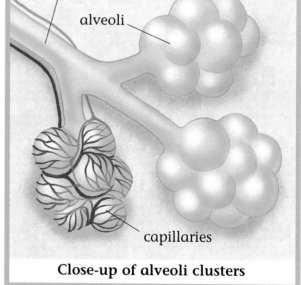

alveoli

capillaries

Close-up of alveoli clusters

Passages and pouches

Air enters your lungs through a network of narrow tubes, called **bronchioles**, that branch away from your two **bronchi**.

At the end of your bronchioles are clusters of tiny air pouches, called **alveoli**. These pass oxygen into your blood and remove waste water and **carbon dioxide**.

If your lungs were simple sacks, their walls wouldn't have a large enough surface area to take in the amount of oxygen you need. That's why you have so many alveoli—about 300 million in each lung.

Although each of your alveoli is less than a thousandth of an inch wide, their total surface area is about half the size of a tennis court.

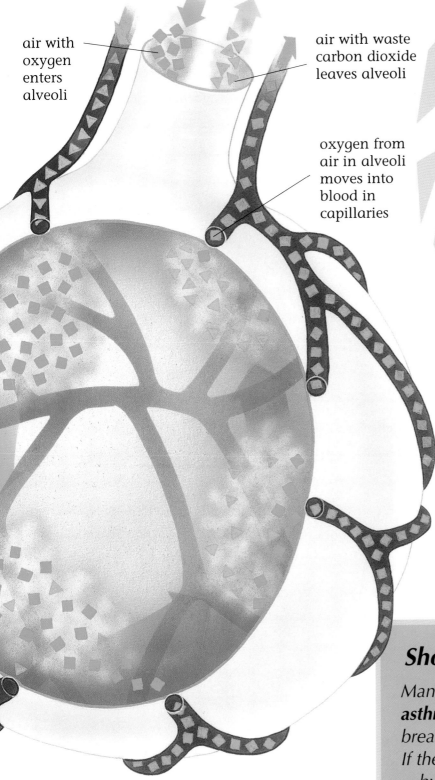

air with oxygen enters alveoli

air with waste carbon dioxide leaves alveoli

oxygen from air in alveoli moves into blood in capillaries

Never empty

Even when you think you're breathing all the way out, your lungs still have lots of air left inside them—easily enough to blow up a small balloon. This makes sure your body has a constant supply of oxygen —even between breaths.

Swapping system

The way the gases move is called **diffusion**. The air that you breathe into your alveoli contains more oxygen than the blood in your capillaries. Some of this oxygen diffuses (drifts through) into your blood to make the balance equal.

In the same way, carbon dioxide passes out of your blood and into your alveoli. This gas leaves your lungs in the air you breathe out.

Short of breath

Many people suffer from **asthma**, which means their breathing system is extrasensitive. If their airways become irritated —by dust, fumes, or a cold, for instance—they make lots of extra **mucus**. At the same time, their bronchioles tighten up, restricting the flow of air into their lungs. This makes them cough and gasp for breath.

Two-way filter

Every cluster of alveoli is covered in blood-carrying tubes called **capillaries**. The walls between them are so thin that gases can easily leak in and out. Oxygen moves out of the alveoli into the blood, while carbon dioxide goes in the opposite direction.

LIQUID LIFELINE

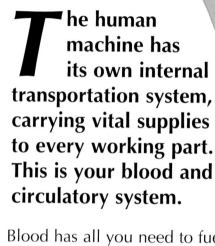

white cells fight germs and diseases

The human machine has its own internal transportation system, carrying vital supplies to every working part. This is your blood and circulatory system.

Blood has all you need to fuel, defend, and patch up your body. Every drop carries life-giving deliveries to all your body **cells**.

Blood also keeps you warm —it takes some heat from busy parts, such as your **heart**, **liver**, and muscles, and sends it to cooler, less active areas, such as your skin.

platelets block cuts

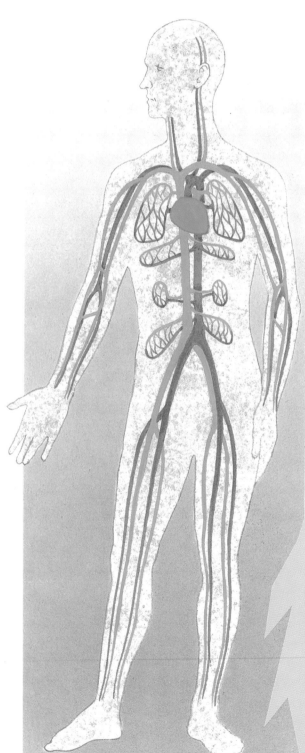

Group matters

Blood may all look the same—but some people's blood is more like yours than others'. Your blood usually fits into one of four main groups—A, B, O or AB. You can donate some of your blood to someone else who needs it— but it will only help them if it's safe to mix your blood type with theirs.

Food flow

less active areas, such as your skin. Blood is runny because just over half of it is a sticky, watery liquid, called **plasma**. **Nutrients** from your food are dissolved in this liquid. Blood carries these chemicals to the body cells that need them.

Oxygen trap

Just under half of your blood is made up of disc-shaped **red blood cells**. A chemical called **hemoglobin** traps **oxygen** from your **lungs** inside these cells—it also gives blood its color.

Red blood cells live only for about four months. Then they are scrapped by your liver. A jelly inside your bones, called **red marrow**, makes new blood cells to replace them—about three million every minute!

Find out how blood makes its deliveries on pages 18-23.

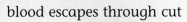

red cells carry oxygen

Pale problem

*Some people don't have enough red cells or hemoglobin in their blood to trap all the oxygen they need. They are suffering from **anemia**. People with anemia often look pale and feel tired. In some cases they can help their bodies make more hemoglobin by eating foods that are rich in a nutrient called **iron**. Red meats and leafy green vegetables are the best sources. Iron tablets may also help.*

Defense and repair

For every 600 red cells, your blood contains one **white blood cell**. These are part of your body's defense system. Most white cells act like mops, swallowing up germs, diseases, and other unwanted objects in your blood. Others act like disinfectants. They make chemicals that attack and destroy harmful materials.

Sticky scraps of cells, called **platelets**, also float in your plasma. If you cut yourself, they will flock to the site of damage and patch it up. The temporary mend they make on the outside of your body is called a scab.

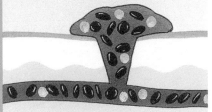

blood escapes through cut

platelets rush to blood in cut to help it plug hole

scab forms to protect skin cells mending underneath

How a cut heals

PAIR OF PUMPS

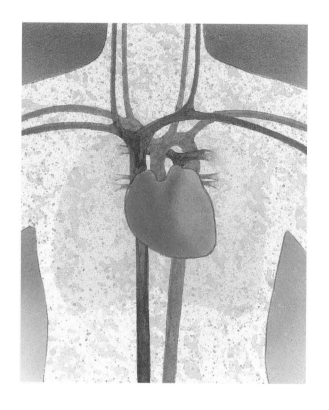

Blood is kept on the move by a powerful pair of pumps. These make up your heart—the center of the human power pack.

Your **heart** pumps blood around your body on an ever-moving circuit. Without this strong, hard-working muscle, your blood's delivery system would grind to a halt.

Your heart is made up of two pumps. The left pump sends blood containing **oxygen** from your **lungs** to all the working parts in your body. The right pump takes in blood that has been around your body and sends it back to your lungs.

One-way system

Each side of your heart is split into two chambers—the **atria** are at the top, and the **ventricles** below. The chambers are separated by **valves**, which stop blood flowing backward through the heart. These valves in action make the familiar "lub-dup" sound of your heartbeat.

Lub

Blood flows from your body into the right atrium, and from your lungs into the left. When both upper chambers are completely full, valves open to let the blood through into the ventricles. As these valves snap shut again, you hear the "lub" sound.

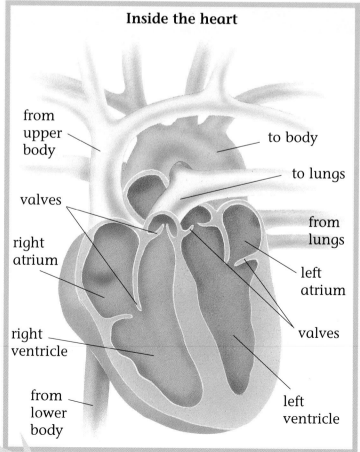

Inside the heart

from upper body

to body

to lungs

valves

from lungs

right atrium

left atrium

valves

right ventricle

left ventricle

from lower body

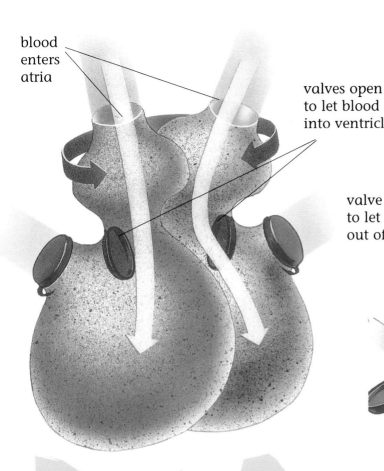

blood enters atria

valves open to let blood into ventricles

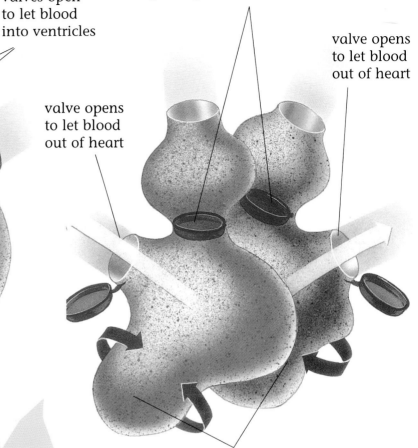

valves close to prevent blood passing back into atria

valve opens to let blood out of heart

valve opens to let blood out of heart

ventricles clench to squeeze blood out of heart

Working life

Imagine how tired you'd be if you clenched then opened your fist once every second for a whole day. Well, your heart has to clench, then relax, around 70 times a minute, every day and night of your life. Amazingly, the average healthy heart can make well over two billion beats in a lifetime.

Dup

The ventricles clench up to squeeze blood out of the heart, and valves at the top of them open to let it through. From the right ventricle it travels to the lungs, and from the left to the rest of the body. "Dup" is the sound of these exit valves closing again.

Keeping time

*If the **nerves** in your heart are damaged, an electronic box called an artificial pacemaker can be fitted under the skin in your shoulder. The box sends tiny pulses of electricity along wires to your heart, 70 to 80 times every minute. These pulses trigger a regular heartbeat. Modern pacemakers have batteries that last for many years.*

CIRCUIT START

arteries carry blood away from heart

Blood travels in a one-way system, away from your heart, all the way around your body then back again. It starts its journey in your arteries.

Round-about route

If you look carefully in the crook of your elbow or at the back of your hands, you may be able to see dark, raised lines under your skin. These are some of your **blood vessels**—the soft, bendy tubes that carry blood around your body.

Vessels that take blood away from your **heart** are called your **arteries**. The ones leading back to your heart are called **veins**. Linking them together is a network of fine tubes, called **capillaries**. These put your blood in contact with your body's **cells**.

Hitching a ride

Blood sends supplies to every cell in your body, so it's a very handy way to give you certain medicines. If a medicine is injected into the blood, it can reach many parts of the body in seconds. In an emergency, pain killers and cures for poison are put into the body in this way.

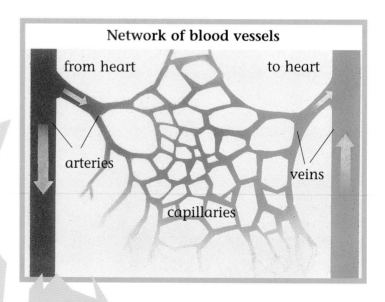

Network of blood vessels

from heart
to heart
arteries
veins
capillaries

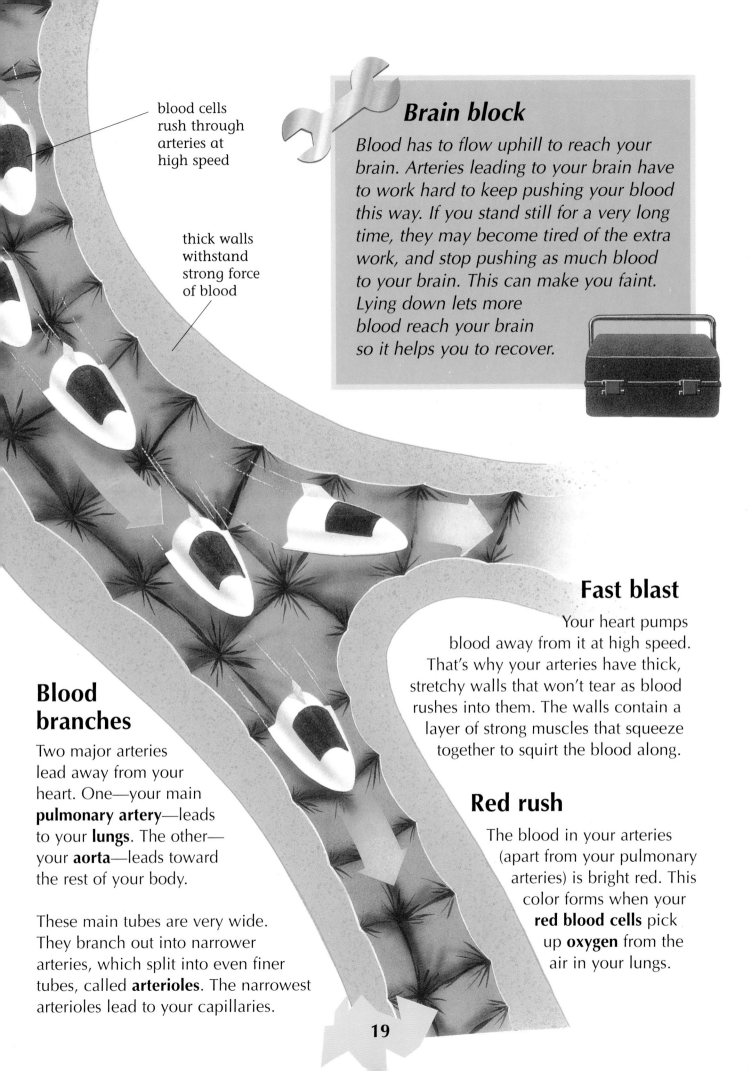

blood cells rush through arteries at high speed

thick walls withstand strong force of blood

Brain block

Blood has to flow uphill to reach your brain. Arteries leading to your brain have to work hard to keep pushing your blood this way. If you stand still for a very long time, they may become tired of the extra work, and stop pushing as much blood to your brain. This can make you faint. Lying down lets more blood reach your brain so it helps you to recover.

Blood branches

Two major arteries lead away from your heart. One—your main **pulmonary artery**—leads to your **lungs**. The other— your **aorta**—leads toward the rest of your body.

These main tubes are very wide. They branch out into narrower arteries, which split into even finer tubes, called **arterioles**. The narrowest arterioles lead to your capillaries.

Fast blast

Your heart pumps blood away from it at high speed. That's why your arteries have thick, stretchy walls that won't tear as blood rushes into them. The walls contain a layer of strong muscles that squeeze together to squirt the blood along.

Red rush

The blood in your arteries (apart from your pulmonary arteries) is bright red. This color forms when your **red blood cells** pick up **oxygen** from the air in your lungs.

FINE FILTERS

A fine filtering system swaps the oxygen in your blood with waste products from your body's cells. This exchange takes place in your capillaries.

Sprinkler system

Blood needs to deliver **oxygen**, **nutrients**, and water to every part of your body. It does this through tiny tubes called **capillaries**. Blood comes to your capillaries from your **arteries**.

Capillaries sprinkle your body **cells** with supplies from your blood. They can do this because they have very thin walls, with tiny slits between the cells. Water, gases, and some chemicals pass through these slits by **diffusion**.

Your capillaries are so narrow that blood cells can only pass through them in single file. This slows down the flow of blood, allowing plenty of time for materials to diffuse between your blood and the surrounding body cells.

capillaries have narrow channel and thin walls

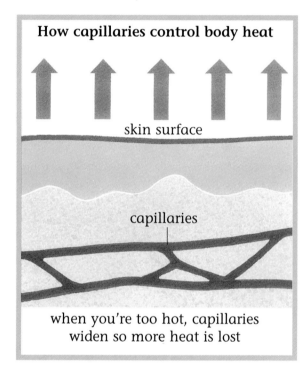

How capillaries control body heat

skin surface

capillaries

when you're too hot, capillaries widen so more heat is lost

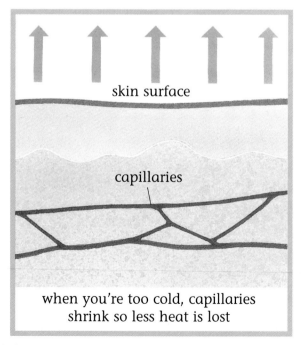

skin surface

capillaries

when you're too cold, capillaries shrink so less heat is lost

Hot and cold

Capillaries in your skin help to control your body temperature. When you're hot, they widen so more blood flows near the skin's surface. This lets more heat escape into the air around you, cooling you down. When you're cold, the capillaries become narrower, letting less blood near the surface. This keeps your heat inside.

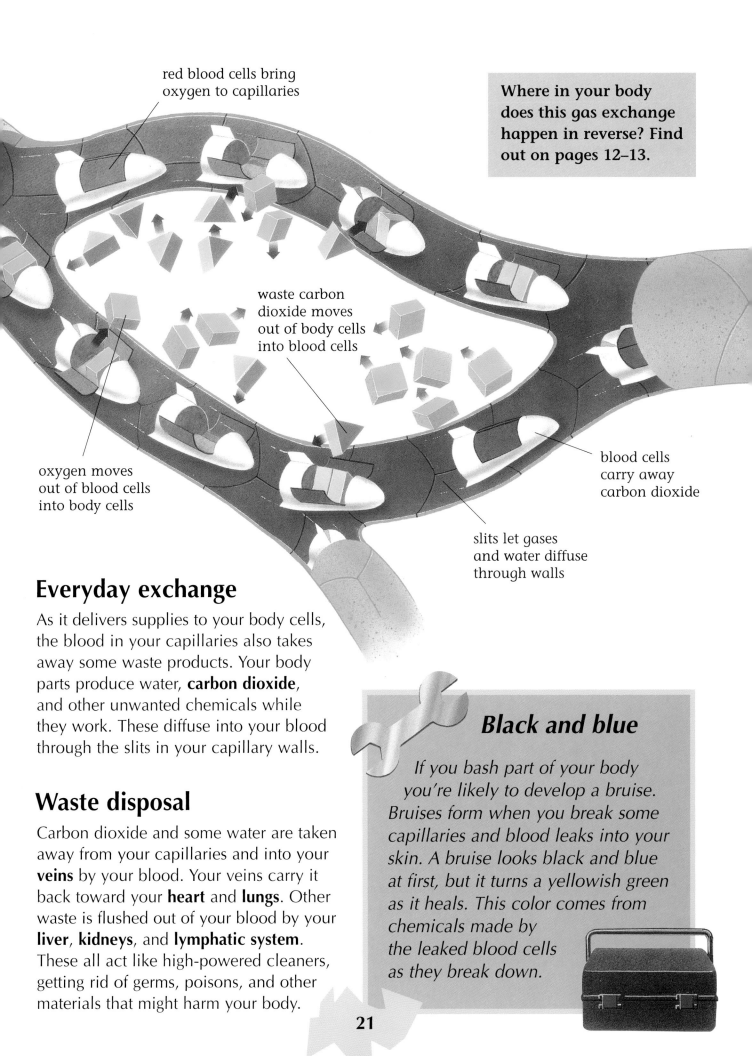

red blood cells bring
oxygen to capillaries

**Where in your body
does this gas exchange
happen in reverse? Find
out on pages 12–13.**

waste carbon
dioxide moves
out of body cells
into blood cells

oxygen moves
out of blood cells
into body cells

blood cells
carry away
carbon dioxide

slits let gases
and water diffuse
through walls

Everyday exchange

As it delivers supplies to your body cells,
the blood in your capillaries also takes
away some waste products. Your body
parts produce water, **carbon dioxide**,
and other unwanted chemicals while
they work. These diffuse into your blood
through the slits in your capillary walls.

Waste disposal

Carbon dioxide and some water are taken
away from your capillaries and into your
veins by your blood. Your veins carry it
back toward your **heart** and **lungs**. Other
waste is flushed out of your blood by your
liver, **kidneys**, and **lymphatic system**.
These all act like high-powered cleaners,
getting rid of germs, poisons, and other
materials that might harm your body.

Black and blue

*If you bash part of your body
you're likely to develop a bruise.
Bruises form when you break some
capillaries and blood leaks into your
skin. A bruise looks black and blue
at first, but it turns a yellowish green
as it heals. This color comes from
chemicals made by
the leaked blood cells
as they break down.*

21

RETURN ROUTE

Blood makes its return trip to the heart through a network of tubes called veins.

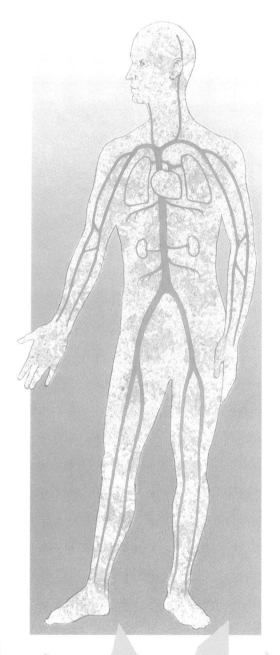

Capillaries leading from your body **cells** gradually join together to form wider tubes, called **venules**. Venules join other venules to form your **veins**.

Veins send blood back toward your **heart**. The veins joining your heart are the widest. The **pulmonary veins** bring your heart blood from your **lungs**. The **superior vena cava** and the **inferior vena cava** carry blood from your upper and lower body.

Purple path

Blood in your veins (except your pulmonary veins) is a dark, purply red. That's because your **red blood cells** have released the **oxygen** that made them bright red, and are now carrying waste **carbon dioxide** from your body's cells.

When this dark red blood reaches your heart, it is pumped straight on to your lungs. Your lungs remove the carbon dioxide, replacing it with oxygen. This makes the blood bright red again.

veins have thin, floppy walls

Plenty to go around

By the time you're fully grown you'll have nearly 62 000 miles of **blood vessels**—enough to stretch almost two-and-a-half times around the equator! Altogether they'll contain around five quarts of blood. About three-fifths of this is in your veins.

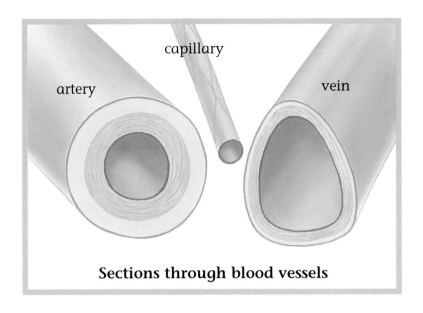

capillary

artery

vein

Sections through blood vessels

No back-flow

Your body muscles squeeze on your veins slightly, helping the blood to move along. Special **valves** keep it going in the right direction. These little flaps close together to stop blood slipping backward. Valves do the most work in places such as your legs, where the blood has to flow a long way uphill.

Steady stream

When blood reaches your veins it has lost most of the pressure from your heart, so your veins don't need to withstand as much force as your **arteries**. Their walls are thinner and floppier. They also have a wider channel for blood to flow through.

valves open
to let blood
flow in right
direction

veins lead
toward
heart

muscles squeeze
on veins to force
blood along

valves close to stop
blood flowing the
wrong way

Lumpy legs

Sometimes the valves in people's veins can start to sag, letting blood flow through them in the wrong direction. As this meets blood flowing the right way, it puts a strain on the walls of the veins, making them bulge. These bulges are called varicose veins. They most often form in people's legs.

PACE OF LIFE

The human power pack is just like a finely-tuned engine. It can pick up speed or slow down as you change the pace of your life.

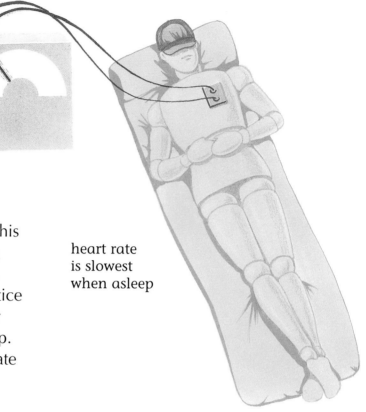

If you're sitting still while you're reading this book, your **heart** will probably be beating quite steadily—around 70 times a minute. But if you start to move around, you'll notice it speeding up. The harder you make your body work, the faster your heart will pump. These illustrations show how your heart rate changes, according to what you're doing.

heart rate is slowest when asleep

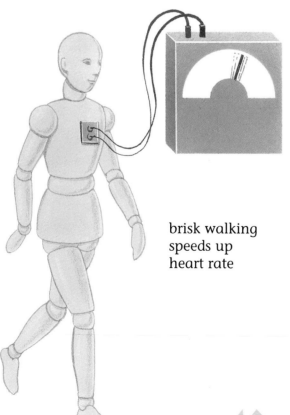

brisk walking speeds up heart rate

All action

When you step up your activity, your body **cells** need more **oxygen** to keep them going. Your heart pumps faster so that your blood can speed up its delivery service. At the same time your **lungs** work harder to take in more oxygen from the air. This makes you breathe much faster and deeper.

Personal pace

Really tough exercise can force your heart to work at three times its normal rate. But the power pack's exact pace depends on the person. Younger, fitter people often have a slower heart rate and steadier breathing than those who are older or don't take much exercise.

Scary business

When something scary happens, we sometimes say we miss a heartbeat. But your heart rate actually increases when you're frightened. That's because your body is preparing to deal with the cause of your fear. It pumps oxygen more quickly around your body so you're ready to fight what's scaring you—or simply run away!

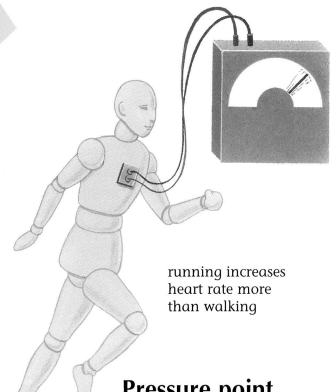

running increases heart rate more than walking

Feel the flow

You can find out how fast your heart is beating by measuring your **pulse**. This is the throbbing you feel if you gently press your fingertips against your inside wrist. It's caused by the spurt of blood that rushes into your **arteries** each time your heart beats.

Pressure point

The force of blood against your artery walls is called your **blood pressure**. Doctors measure it to gauge how tightly the blood is packed into your arteries. Two pressures are recorded. The first is when your heart has just pumped blood into your arteries and they are full. The second is taken as your heart is refilling, when your arteries contain the smallest amount of blood.

hard exercise can more than double heart rate

High pressure

If someone has high blood pressure, their heart has to work extra hard to pump the blood around their body. High blood pressure may be a sign of illness, stress or too much body weight. It can be a dangerous condition.

CARE AND SERVICING

You need to look after your power pack if you want it to last a long lifetime. Luckily, caring for your power pack is both cheap and easy.

Keep it pumping

Many ordinary engines wear out faster if you use them a lot. But the more you use your power pack, the better it gets. Swimming, cycling, playing baseball, and other gentle exercise will all help to keep your **heart**, **lungs**, and **circulation** in good shape. If you do this at least a couple of times a week, your power pack will be able to run better than ever.

Keep it clear

Fat gets into your blood when your body breaks down the food you eat. You need some fat to give you energy—but if you eat too much, your blood may leave traces of it inside your **arteries**. This clogs them up, making it hard for your heart to pump blood through them. A blocked artery is dangerous. As well as causing high **blood pressure**, it could lead to a heart attack or a **stroke**.

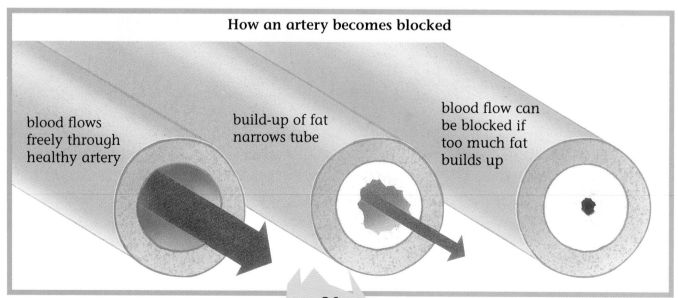

How an artery becomes blocked

blood flows freely through healthy artery

build-up of fat narrows tube

blood flow can be blocked if too much fat builds up

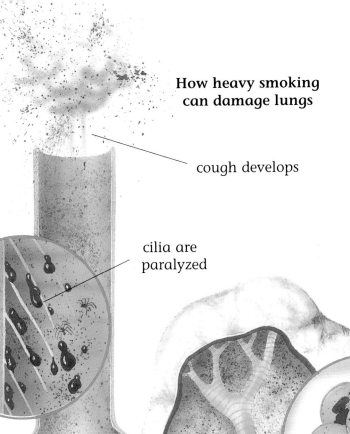

How heavy smoking can damage lungs

cough develops

cilia are paralyzed

alveoli fill with tar

bronchioles stiffen with mucus

very bad coughing can burst alveoli

No smoking

People who care about their power packs should avoid smoking at all costs. Cigarette smoke is deadly poison to the human machine. It paralyzes **cilia**, and clogs up lungs and airways with **mucus** and tar. It can also lead to **cancer**.

Losing elastic

Smokers often develop a cough because their airways become irritated. Coughing produces extra mucus, which thickens the lining of their **bronchioles** and makes them stiff. This makes it hard for the bronchioles to absorb the force of air as they cough. It puts extra pressure on their **alveoli**—sometimes enough to burst them. Damaged alveoli make it very difficult to breathe.

Risky business

Smoking doesn't only affect your lungs. It can also clog up **blood vessels** and may seriously damage your heart.

Dangerous drink

Large amounts of alcohol can damage the muscles in your heart. It can also lead to high blood pressure. It's best not to drink too much alcohol if you want your power pack to carry on working well.

Back to life

If a person's power pack stops working suddenly—in an accident, for instance—there's a small chance that someone else could make it start again. This is called **resuscitation**. You can learn how to resuscitate people in an emergency by taking a first-aid course.

27

OTHER MODELS

Your heart and lungs may work well for you—but the human power pack is not the only model around. Many other animals have very different breathing and circulatory systems.

Airy insects

Humans couldn't breathe without **lungs** —but an insect has no lungs at all. Air moves around an insect's body through a network of tubes, called tracheoles. These tubes lead to tiny openings, called spiracles, on the outside of the insect's body. The holes act like mini air vents, bringing the insect a continual supply of life-giving **oxygen**.

Plenty of pumps

You may have only one **heart**—but a worm has ten! They're not complicated pumps like ours—instead each one is just a muscly bulge in a main **blood vessel**. The bulges lie in pairs along the sides of the worm's body. They each squeeze on the blood to push it around.

Two-way toads

Toads are amphibians—creatures that can survive both underwater and in air. They can either soak up oxygen through their skin, or by using their lungs.

True blue

Not all blood is red. A lobster's blood is greenish blue. That's because it contains a chemical full of copper, instead of **hemoglobin**.

An insect's power pack

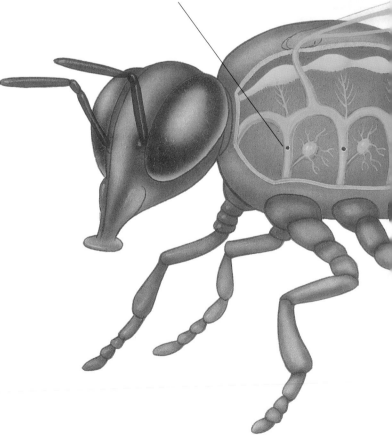

air moves in and out through small holes

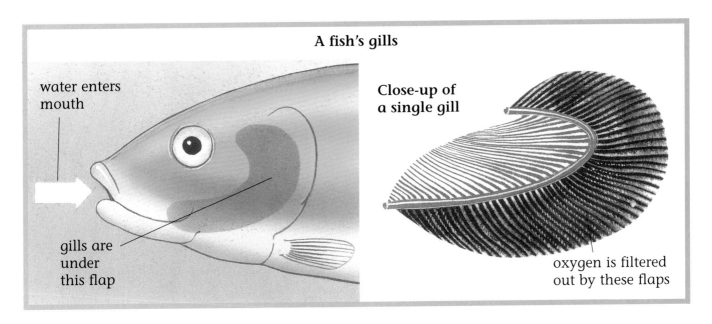

A fish's gills

water enters mouth

gills are under this flap

Close-up of a single gill

oxygen is filtered out by these flaps

Fishy filters

Because fish live in water, they don't breathe in air at all. Their oxygen comes from the water itself. When a fish swims along, it takes in water through its mouth. The water is forced through special flaps, called gills, in the side of the fish's head. These filter out the oxygen and pass it into their blood.

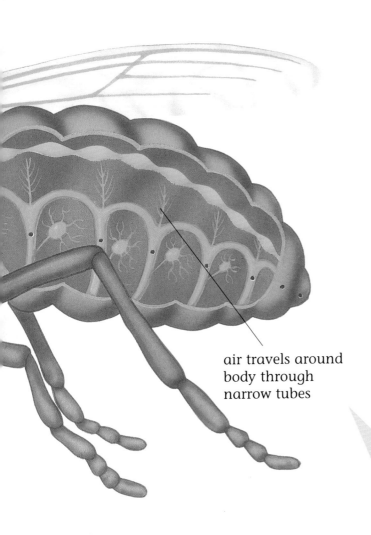

air travels around body through narrow tubes

Big breath

Imagine being able to hold your breath for over an hour—that's what whales can do. When a whale comes to the surface of the sea it breathes in air through one or two tiny holes on the top of its head. It can then hold its breath for a very long time while it swims underwater. A whale can spend up to 75 minutes below the surface, surviving on the oxygen stored in its blood and lungs.

GLOSSARY

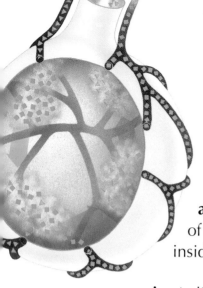

alveoli The millions of tiny, moist air pouches inside your lungs.

anemia A disease caused by a lack of iron in the blood.

aorta The main artery that leads from your heart to your body.

arteries Tubes that carry blood from your heart to all parts of your body.

arterioles The narrowest arteries.

asthma A disease that makes people short of breath.

atria The upper chambers of your heart.

blood pressure A measure of the blood in your arteries that shows how hard your heart is working.

blood vessels The many tubes that carry blood around your body.

bronchi The two airways that connect your trachea to your lungs.

bronchioles The thousands of airways that branch out from your bronchi.

cancer A disease that forms lumps called tumors which stop organs working properly.

capillaries Tiny blood-carrying tubes with leaky walls.

carbon dioxide A gas that your cells produce as a waste product. It leaves your body when you breathe out.

cartilage A strong but slightly squashy material that helps to protect parts of the body and gives them shape.

cells The billions of very tiny parts that combine to make up your body tissues.

cilia Fine hairs that line the nasal cavity, trachea, and other parts of the body.

circulation The journey of your blood around your body.

diaphragm The muscle that moves up and down to force air in and out of your lungs.

diffusion The way liquids and gases move.

epiglottis The fleshy trap door that can close over the opening of your trachea.

exhale To breathe out.

hemoglobin The chemical in your red blood cells that traps oxygen, giving blood its color.

heart The organ that pumps blood around your body.

inferior vena cava The vein that brings blood from your lower body to your heart.

inhale To breathe in.

iron A metal and nutrient that helps make hemoglobin in your red blood cells.

kidneys Two organs that help flush out waste products from your blood.

larynx The bulging tube at the top of your trachea that contains your vocal cords.

liver An organ that makes and stores chemicals and cleans some poisons and worn-out cells from your blood.

lungs The two sponge-like organs in your chest that fill with air when you breathe in.

lymphatic system A system that destroys some germs and unwanted waste products from your cells.

mucus The slime that lines your airways.

nasal cavity The hollow behind your nose.

nerves Fine threads that carry messages between your brain and other body parts.

nutrients The chemical substances in food that your body needs to survive.

oxygen A gas that makes up about a fifth of the air around us. Our cells need it to break down chemicals and release energy.

pharynx The airway that connects the mouth and nose to the trachea and the tube that leads to the stomach.

plasma The straw-colored, watery liquid that makes up about half of your blood.

platelets Sticky cells that help mend blood vessels when you cut yourself.

pulmonary arteries The arteries that lead from your heart to your lungs.

pulmonary veins The veins that lead from your lungs to your heart.

pulse The throbbing of blood against the walls of your arteries.

red blood cells The cells that carry oxygen around your body.

red marrow The jelly inside your bones that makes and stores red blood cells.

resuscitation The emergency technique used to restart the heart and breathing.

stroke Damage to the brain caused by a blocked or burst artery.

superior vena cava The vein that carries blood from your upper body to your heart.

trachea The airway that connects your pharynx to your lungs.

valves Flaps that stop blood flowing the wrong way through a tube.

veins Tubes taking blood to the heart.

ventricles The lower chambers of your heart.

venules The narrowest veins.

vocal cords Two flaps of skin that vibrate to make sounds.

white blood cells Cells that attack germs and harmful objects in your blood.

31

INDEX